Games Around the World

# Card Games

by Dana Meachen Rau

Content Adviser: John McLeod, International Playing-Card Society, London, England
Reading Adviser: Rosemary G. Palmer, Ph.D., Department of Literacy,
College of Education, Boise State University

COMPASS POINT BOOKS ✦ MINNEAPOLIS, MINNESOTA

Compass Point Books
3109 West 50th Street, #115
Minneapolis, MN 55410

Visit Compass Point Books on the Internet at *www.compasspointbooks.com* or
e-mail your request to *custserv@compasspointbooks.com*

Photographs ©: Gary Sundermeyer, cover; Andres Hernandez/Liaison/
Getty Images, 4; Photri-Microstock/Jeff Greenberg, 5; Vancouver Museum
Collection, 6; SEF/Art Resource, N.Y., 9; George Disario/Corbis, 13; Tom &
Dee Ann McCarthy/Corbis, 19; Doug Crouch/Corbis, 25; Wolfgang Kaehler/
Corbis, 27.

Creative Director: Terri Foley
Managing Editor: Catherine Neitge
Editor: Jennifer VanVoorst
Photo Researcher: Svetlana Zhurkina
Designer: Bradfordesign, Inc.
Illustrator and page production: Jaime Martens
Educational Consultant: Diane Smolinski

**Library of Congress Cataloging-in-Publication Data**
Rau, Dana Meachen, 1971–
   Card games / by Dana Meachen Rau.
    v. cm. — (Games around the world)
   Includes bibliographical references and index.
   Contents: Hundreds of games—History of cards—What's in a deck?—
Card playing basics—P'yanitsa: a game from Russia—Go fish—
Solitaire: the royal palace—Building a card house—Cards around the world—
Glossary—Did you know?—Want to know more?
   ISBN 0-7565-0675-1 (hardcover)
    1. Card games—Juvenile literature. [1. Card games. 2. Games.] I. Title. II. Series.
GV1244.R38 2005
795.4—dc22                           2003024092

# Table of Contents

NOTE: *In this book, words that are defined in the glossary are in* **bold** *the first time they appear in the text.*

# Hundreds of Games

Have you ever packed for a trip? It is sometimes hard to fit everything you need into a suitcase. What if you wanted to bring games to keep you busy on vacation? How many do you think you could fit in your suitcase?

▲ *You can play solitaire games by yourself—even on an airplane!*

Would you believe that you can fit hundreds of games in just one pocket? You can with a pack of cards. There are hundreds of different card games. You can play **solitaire** games by yourself, or you can play many other games with one or more friends. All you need to play these games is a **deck** of cards and a flat surface to play them on.

◀ *Card games are a fun way to spend time when traveling.*

# The History of Cards

People have played with cards for a very long time. Historians believe card games were first played in China around the 12th century because China is where paper was first invented. Chinese cards had suits, or groups of cards, based on different money values, and featured pictures of coins and other items.

Card games spread across Asia to Arab countries. European explorers passing through these areas found out about the new games and brought the ideas home with them. Card games were being played in some European countries by the 1370s.

At first, cards were made by hand, so a deck was very expensive. Card makers later used **woodcuts** to stamp the pictures on the cards. When the **printing press** was invented in the 1400s, cards became less costly because they could be made more quickly and easily. Since more people could afford to buy cards, more people began to play card games.

◀ *A deck of Chinese playing cards*

The French are very important in the history of cards. The cards they played with had pictures of hearts, diamonds, clubs, and spades on their faces, or fronts. By the 1500s, these pictures were the ones used on most playing cards, perhaps because they were the easiest to print with a printing press.

In the 1800s, Americans made some changes to playing cards. They made the picture cards two-headed so that they looked the same upside down or right-side up. They also added small numbers and letters to the corners of the cards so that players would easily know what cards they held during a game.

The cards we use today look a little different from cards of long ago, but they have not changed very much. Many of the games we play today are the same as ones that have been played for hundreds of years. New games are created all the time, too. People around the world play all of these games, old and new, together.

*Making playing cards in France, around 1680* ▶

# What's in a Deck?

A set of cards is called a deck. Each deck has 52 cards. On their back sides, all cards look the same, but on their fronts, or faces, each card looks different. There are four suits, or groups of cards, in a deck—spades, clubs, diamonds, and hearts. Spades and clubs are black. Diamonds and hearts are red. There are 13 cards in each suit.

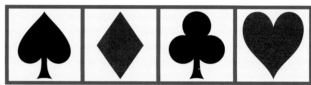

▲ The four suits, from left, are spades, diamonds, clubs, and hearts.

Each suit has number cards. They are numbered from 2 to 10. Each one has a number in the corner and the same number of **pips** in the center of the card. A pip is the symbol used for spades, clubs, diamonds, and hearts.

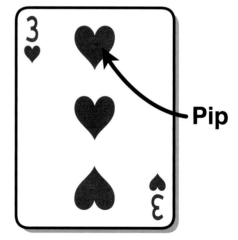

**Pip**

▲ There are three heart pips in the center of the 3 of hearts card.

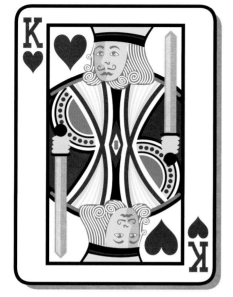

▲ *The three face cards, from left, are king, queen, and jack.*

Each suit also has three cards called **face cards**. They show the faces of a king, a queen, and a jack on them. There is also a card called an ace. The cards, from lowest to highest value, are 2, 3, 4, 5, 6, 7, 8, 9, 10, jack, queen, king, and ace. Although the ace is usually the highest card, the ace acts as a 1 in some games and so becomes the lowest card.

Some decks also have two cards called jokers. They are only used in a few games. When jokers are part of a deck, the deck has 54 cards.

# Card Playing Basics

Before you start a game, you have to be sure the cards are shuffled. Shuffling the cards mixes all the suits together.

**Here's how to shuffle:**

1. **Cut** the deck into two facedown stacks.

2. Take one stack of cards in each hand. Put your thumbs under the ends of each stack.

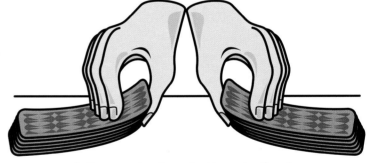

▲ *Put your thumbs under the ends of each stack and release the cards as you press the stacks together.*

3. Start letting go of the cards at the bottom while gently pushing the stacks together. The cards will mix together.

After the deck is shuffled, you have to **deal** cards to each player. The **dealer** starts with the person on his or her left and then moves around the circle, giving each player a card facedown. The dealer deals his or her own card last. Then the dealer passes out cards around the circle again and again until each player has the right number of cards for the game being played.

The cards a player holds are called his or her hand. In most games, players hold their hands so that they can see the faces of the cards but other players cannot. To look at another player's cards is usually considered cheating.

▲ *Don't show the other players your cards!*

# P'yanitsa—A Game from Russia

The object of P'yanitsa is to get rid of all of your cards. You need two players and only 36 cards—all of the aces, kings, queens, jacks, 10s, 9s, 8s, 7s, and 6s. In this game, aces are the highest card and 6s are the lowest, but if a 6 and an ace are played together, the 6 is higher.

1. Shuffle the cards. Then cut the deck in half, making sure that players each receive a stack of 18 cards placed facedown in front of them.

2. At the same time, players place the top card from their stacks faceup in the middle.

14

▲ *Each player turns over his or her top card and places it in the middle.*

3. The player whose card is higher takes both cards and places them facedown at the bottom of his or her stack.

4. If both cards are of equal value, players place one card facedown and one faceup on top of their original faceup card. The player with the new higher card takes all the cards.

5. Keep playing until one person has all the cards and the other has none. The person with no cards is the winner.

▲ When both cards are of equal value, two new cards must be played.

15

# Go Fish

The object of Go Fish is to collect the most sets of four of a kind—for example, all four kings, all four 5s, etc. You need two to six players.

**Here's how to play:**

1. If there are two players, deal seven cards to each. If there are more than two players, deal out five cards to each. Place the remaining cards in a facedown **draw pile** in the center.

Player 3

Draw Pile

Player 2

Player 4

Player 1

2. The player to the dealer's left goes first. This player, Player 1, asks another player for one of the same cards she is holding in her hand. She might say, "Marco, do you have any 3s?"

3. If Marco has one 3, or more than one 3, he has to give them all to Player 1.

4. Player 1 continues with her turn. She can ask Marco if he has a different card, or she can ask another player for 3s, or a different card. For example, "Allison, do you have any 3s?"

5. If Allison does not have any 3s, Allison says, "No. Go fish."

6. Player 1 takes a card from the draw pile. If the card is a 3, she shows it to the others and can keep asking for cards. If it is not a 3, she puts it in her hand, and it is the next player's turn.

7. Play continues around the table as players try to collect sets of four cards of the same **rank**. If a player gets four of a kind, he or she places the cards on the table. It is the end of that player's turn, and the next player gets to go.

8. If a player runs out of cards when there are still more cards in the draw pile, he or she draws five more cards so that play can continue.

9. When the draw pile is gone and players are all out of cards, the game is over.

10. Players count their sets of four cards. The player with the most sets of four is the winner.

*Go Fish is a fun game to play with friends or family.* ▶

# Solitaire—The Royal Palace

The object of The Royal Palace is to place all of the kings, queens, and jacks in their proper "rooms" in the "palace." Suits do not matter in this game—as long as a king is in a king spot, a queen in a queen spot, and a jack in a jack spot, it doesn't matter what suits they are. As with all solitaire games, you are the only player you need!

You will win if you can put each king, queen, and jack in its correct room, with no cards in the center, like this:

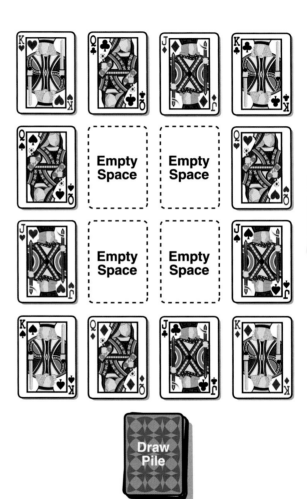

**Here's how to play:**

1.  Deal out the 16 cards faceup to make four rows of four cards per row. Each card you deal may be placed anywhere in the 16 spaces of the palace. For example, if you draw a queen, you'll want to put her in an empty queen spot, if there is one. (At any time if you draw a 10, place it in your **discard pile** and put a new card in the palace instead.)

2.  Now it is time to discard the cards you don't need. You do this by taking out pairs of cards that add up to 10. The ace is a 1 in this game, so these pairs are the ace and 9, 2 and 8, 3 and 7, 4 and 6, and 5 and 5. Take out these pairs and put them in your discard pile. Try to clear the outer rooms first to make room for the kings, queens, and jacks.

3. Now start flipping cards from your draw pile again into your empty spaces. Try not to block king, queen, and jack spots right away. It might be better to fill up the four center spots if they are empty before taking rooms away from the face cards. You never know if the next card you flip will be a face card that needs a spot.

4. Continue filling in the spots and then taking out the pairs. You win if you can put each king, queen, and jack in its correct room with no cards in the center.

5. If at any time you draw a king, queen, or jack, and you do not have a proper room for it at the palace, the game is over and you need to start again.

# Building a Card House

You have to be very careful and patient to build a card house, but it can be a lot of fun. All you need is a deck of cards and a flat table or floor. You can use more decks if you want to make your house very large. You can play with a friend and make it into a game.

**Here's how to build a house:**

1. You need to work together! Hold a card with its long edge on the tabletop while the other player leans the middle of his or her card on the short end of your card. The two cards leaning against each other should look like the capital letter T.

▲ Lean two cards together to form a capital T.

2. Then lean another card at the other end of the first card so that the cards look like a capital letter I.

3. Then the other player leans the next card on the end of any of the cards on the table.

4. You and the other player take turns placing cards and watching your house grow.

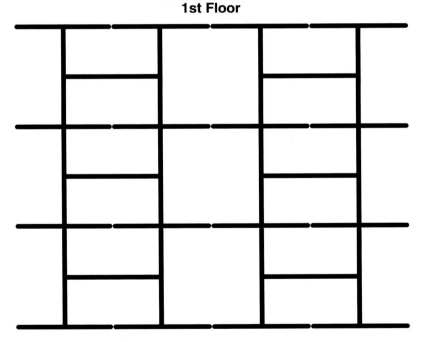

**Overhead View
1st Floor**

▲ *Create the first floor of your house by placing your cards in a pattern like this.*

5. When the first floor of your house seems big enough, start on a second floor! Lay cards flat on top of the other cards like a roof. This creates the floor for the next layer.

6. Again, begin with a T shape, and then start putting up more walls.

7. Continue placing cards until you run out—or until your house topples over!

▲ Be very careful when you place your cards!

Before you start building, be sure to close the window! Even the slightest breeze could send your house crashing to the ground.

# Cards Around the World

As you play card games or build a card house with your friends, think about people in other parts of the world. They might be playing cards with their friends, too.

People play card games from the islands of New Zealand to the deserts of Egypt. They play in chilly Norway and in the sunny Caribbean. People may play with different kinds of decks. Sometimes decks are different from country to country. A Spanish deck has 40 cards. Russians play many games with 36 cards. In India, a small number of players play with Ganjifa cards. These cards are round in shape with up to 144 cards in a deck.

There are many different kinds of cards and card games, and they are not exactly alike from place to place. Their purpose, though, is always the same—to have fun!

*These friends in Panama enjoy ▶*
*playing a game outside.*

# Glossary

**cut**—to divide the deck into two parts

**deal**—to give out cards to the other players

**dealer**—the person who gives out the cards to the other players

**deck**—a complete set of cards

**discard pile**—a pile that contains cards you have removed from your hand

**draw pile**—a pile from which you take cards to add to your hand

**face cards**—the king, queen, and jack cards

**pips**—the small symbols on the number cards

**printing press**—a machine that is able to create many copies of one picture or document

**rank**—cards grouped by face or number; there are four cards of each rank.

**solitaire**—a card game with only one player

**woodcuts**—pieces of wood carved with an image that can be stamped onto paper to make many copies of one picture

# Did You Know?

Playing cards have been used throughout Europe as money when metal and paper were in short supply.

In France, the suit of clubs is called *trèfles,* which means "clovers." In Spain, the word for that suit is *bastos,* which means "clubs." The name from Spain became mixed up with the picture from France. Today, the picture for clubs looks like a clover.

In medieval times, a deck of cards was considered so special that decks were often given as wedding presents.

Americans invented the joker card in the 1860s. Decks in North America have two jokers, but European decks usually have three.

Some of the earliest hand-made cards were beautifully decorated. Many of them were painted with gold paint.

Many cards used today in parts of Germany feature suits of hearts, bells, leaves, and acorns. Spanish and Latin American suits are commonly money, cups, swords, and clubs.

# Want to Know More?

### At the Library

Eagle, Terry. *Kids' Card Games.* Hauppauge, N.Y.: Barrons, 2002.

Golick, Margie. *Card Games for Smart Kids.* New York: Sterling Publications, 1999.

Maccoll, Gail. *The Book of Card Games for Little Kids.* New York: Workman Publishing Company, 2000.

### On the Web

For more information on card games, use FactHound
to track down Web sites related to this book.

1. Go to *www.facthound.com*
2. Type in a search word related to this book
   or this book ID: 0756506751
3. Click on the *Fetch It* button.

Your trusty FactHound will fetch the best Web sites for you!

## On the Road

**Beinecke Rare Book and Manuscript Library**
Yale University Campus
P.O. Box 208240
New Haven, CT 06520
To see a very large collection of playing cards from countries all over
the world, as well as the printing materials used to make them

**Elliot Avedon Museum and Archive of Games**
University of Waterloo
200 University Ave.
Waterloo, Ontario N2L 3G1
Canada
519/888-4567
To see a collection of playing cards and related equipment from
countries all over the world

# Index

## About the Author

Dana Meachen Rau is an author, editor, and illustrator.
A graduate of Trinity College in Hartford, Connecticut,
she has written more than 90 books for children,
including nonfiction, biographies, early readers,
and historical fiction. Ms. Rau plays card games
with her kids on the floor, and with her husband
at the kitchen table. She lives in Burlington,
Connecticut, with her husband, Chris, and her
children, Charlie and Allison.